Made in the USA
Columbia, SC
12 March 2025

55070488R00057